BITCOIN INVESTMENT STRATEGY FOR BEGINNERS

A Beginners Guide to Building Wealth in the World of Cryptocurrency

REBELLO M. POSTON

Copyright

All rights reserved. No part of this publication may be reproduced, distributed, or transmitted in any form or by any means, including photocopying, recording, or other electronic or mechanical methods, without the prior written permission of the publisher, except in the case of brief quotations embodied in critical reviews and certain other noncommercial uses permitted by copyright law.

Copyright© Rebello M. Poston, 2024.

TABLE OF CONTENTS

INTRODUCTION

CHAPTER 1: BASICS OF BITCOIN
- What is Bitcoin?
- History of Bitcoin
- How Bitcoin Works
- Importance of Bitcoin in the Modern Economy

CHAPTER 2: UNDERSTANDING THE BASICS OF BITCOIN INVESTMENT
- Why Invest in Bitcoin?
- Risk and Reward in Bitcoin Investment
- Common Myths and Misconceptions
- Legal and Regulatory Considerations

CHAPTER 3: SETTING UP FOR BITCOIN INVESTMENT
- Choosing the Right Bitcoin Wallet
- Setting Up a Secure Wallet
- Understanding Bitcoin Exchanges
- Steps to Buying Your First Bitcoin

CHAPTER 4: DEVELOPING YOUR INVESTMENT STRATEGY
- Defining Your Investment Goals
- Long-Term vs. Short-Term Investment
- Diversifying Your Bitcoin Portfolio
- Managing Risks and Volatility

CHAPTER 5: ANALYZING THE MARKET
- Reading Bitcoin Charts
- Technical Analysis Basics
- Fundamental Analysis of Bitcoin
- Staying Informed with News and Trends

CHAPTER 6: BEST PRACTICES AND FUTURE TRENDS
- Best Practices for Safe Investing
- Common Mistakes to Avoid
- The Future of Bitcoin and Cryptocurrencies
- Preparing for the Long Haul

CONCLUSION

INTRODUCTION

Whether you're entirely new to Bitcoin or have a basic understanding and want to deepen your knowledge, this book is designed to guide you through the essentials of investing in this revolutionary digital currency. As Bitcoin continues to capture the imagination of the financial world, more and more individuals are exploring its potential as a viable investment. This guide aims to equip you with the knowledge and strategies needed to navigate the complexities of Bitcoin investment with confidence.

Bitcoin, often referred to as digital gold, has emerged as a unique asset class with the potential for high returns, but also comes with significant risks. Understanding what Bitcoin is, how it operates, and why it holds value is crucial before diving into the investment aspects. In this book, we'll start with the basics, explaining the history and technology behind Bitcoin, and gradually build up to more advanced topics like market analysis and investment strategies.

Investing in Bitcoin is not merely about buying and holding. It requires a strategic approach, awareness of market trends, and a clear understanding of your investment goals and risk tolerance. This book will help you define these elements, offering practical advice on creating a secure wallet, choosing the right exchanges, and making informed investment decisions.

Moreover, the world of Bitcoin is constantly evolving, with new developments and regulatory changes shaping its landscape. Staying informed and adaptable is key to successful investing. We'll cover best practices, common pitfalls to avoid, and future trends that could impact your investments.

By the end of this book, you should feel confident in your ability to invest in Bitcoin smartly and safely. Whether you're looking to make your first purchase or refine your existing strategy, "Bitcoin Investment Strategy for Beginners" is your comprehensive guide to understanding and investing in Bitcoin. Let's embark on this journey together, unlocking the potential of Bitcoin and paving the way for your financial growth.

CHAPTER 1: BASICS OF BITCOIN

WHAT IS BITCOIN?

Bitcoin is a decentralized digital currency that operates on a peer-to-peer network, allowing users to conduct transactions without the need for intermediaries such as banks or financial institutions. Introduced in 2009 by an anonymous person or group of people using the pseudonym Satoshi Nakamoto, Bitcoin was designed to offer an alternative to traditional fiat currencies and provide a new form of financial autonomy.

At its core, Bitcoin is based on blockchain technology, a distributed ledger that records all transactions across a network of computers. This ledger is secured through cryptographic techniques, ensuring the integrity and immutability of transaction data. Each transaction is grouped into a "block" and added to a chain of previous transactions, hence the term "blockchain."

Bitcoin's decentralized nature means it is not controlled by any central authority or government, which is a fundamental departure from traditional financial systems. This decentralization is achieved through a consensus mechanism known as "proof of work," where network participants, called miners, use computational power to solve complex mathematical problems that validate transactions and add new blocks to the blockchain. As a reward for their efforts, miners receive newly minted bitcoins.

One of the key features of Bitcoin is its limited supply. The total number of bitcoins that will ever be created is capped at 21 million, making it a deflationary asset. This scarcity, combined with increasing demand, has contributed to Bitcoin's reputation as "digital gold" and a store of value.

Bitcoin can be used for various purposes, including purchasing goods and services, transferring value across borders, and as an investment. Its value can be volatile, influenced by factors such as market demand, regulatory news, technological developments, and macroeconomic trends.

Overall, Bitcoin represents a significant innovation in the financial world, offering a new paradigm for digital transactions and investment. Understanding its underlying technology and principles is essential for anyone looking to invest or participate in the Bitcoin ecosystem.

HISTORY OF BITCOIN

The history of Bitcoin is a tale of innovation, speculation, and a quest for a decentralized form of currency. It all began in 2008 when a whitepaper titled "Bitcoin: A Peer-to-Peer Electronic Cash System" was published by an unknown person or group of people using the pseudonym Satoshi Nakamoto. The whitepaper outlined a system that would allow for direct transactions between parties without the need for a trusted third party, using cryptographic proof instead of trust.

In January 2009, Nakamoto released the first Bitcoin software, launching the network by mining the genesis block, also known as Block 0. Embedded in this block was a message, "The Times 03/Jan/2009 Chancellor on brink of second bailout for banks," referencing a headline about the financial crisis, underscoring Bitcoin's purpose as an alternative to traditional financial systems.

The first real-world transaction using Bitcoin occurred in May 2010 when a programmer named Laszlo Hanyecz paid 10,000 bitcoins for two pizzas. This event, known as "Bitcoin Pizza Day," highlighted Bitcoin's potential as a medium of exchange, despite its initially low value.

Bitcoin began to gain more attention and users in 2011 when its price reached parity with the US dollar. During this period, alternative cryptocurrencies, or "altcoins," began to emerge, inspired by Bitcoin's open-source code. However, Bitcoin's rise was not without challenges. The infamous Silk Road, an online marketplace that used Bitcoin for illegal transactions, was shut down by the FBI in 2013, bringing negative publicity and regulatory scrutiny to the nascent cryptocurrency.

Despite these setbacks, Bitcoin continued to grow. By 2013, its price had surged to over $1,000, driven by increasing interest from investors and media coverage. However, this rapid growth also led to bubbles and subsequent crashes, highlighting the currency's volatility.

In the following years, Bitcoin saw significant developments and wider adoption. Major companies like Microsoft and Overstock began accepting Bitcoin as payment. The launch of Bitcoin futures by major financial exchanges in 2017 marked its entry into the mainstream financial markets, further legitimizing it as an asset class.

The most dramatic price surge occurred in late 2017, when Bitcoin reached nearly $20,000 per coin, driven by speculative investment and growing public interest. However, the bubble burst in early 2018, and the price plummeted, demonstrating the high-risk nature of Bitcoin investment.

In recent years, Bitcoin has continued to mature. Institutional investors, including hedge funds and publicly traded companies, have started to invest in Bitcoin, viewing it as a hedge against inflation and economic uncertainty. Developments such as the Lightning Network aim to improve Bitcoin's scalability and transaction speed, addressing some of its technical limitations.

Bitcoin's journey from a whitepaper to a trillion-dollar market cap has been marked by innovation, controversy, and growing acceptance. Its history is a testament to the disruptive potential of decentralized technologies and their ability to reshape the financial landscape.

HOW BITCOIN WORKS

Bitcoin operates on a decentralized network that allows for peer-to-peer transactions without the need for intermediaries such as banks. This innovative system is underpinned by several key technologies and concepts:

1. Blockchain Technology: At the core of Bitcoin is blockchain technology, a distributed ledger that records all transactions across a network of computers, known as nodes. The blockchain is a chain of blocks, with each block containing a list of recent transactions. Once a block is completed, it is added to the chain, creating a permanent and unalterable record.

2. Decentralization and Peer-to-Peer Network: Bitcoin's network is decentralized, meaning no single entity controls it. Instead, it operates on a peer-to-peer basis, with each participant (node) having a copy of the entire blockchain. This decentralization ensures that the system is resilient and resistant to censorship or fraud.

3. Cryptographic Security: Bitcoin uses cryptographic techniques to secure transactions. Each user has a pair of cryptographic keys: a public key, which is their address on the network, and a private key, which is kept secret and used to sign transactions. This ensures that only the owner of the private key can spend the associated bitcoins.

4. Mining and Proof of Work: New bitcoins are created through a process called mining, which involves solving complex mathematical problems using computational power. Miners compete to solve these problems, and the first to find a solution adds a new block to the blockchain and is rewarded with newly minted bitcoins and transaction fees. This process is known as proof of work and is fundamental to the security and integrity of the network.

5. Transactions: A Bitcoin transaction involves transferring value from one address to another. When a user initiates a transaction, it is broadcast to the network, where miners verify its validity and include it in a new block. Transactions are confirmed once they are added to the blockchain, and the more confirmations a transaction has, the more secure it is considered.

6. Limited Supply: Bitcoin's supply is capped at 21 million coins, a feature hardcoded into its protocol. This scarcity is designed to mimic precious metals like gold, making Bitcoin a deflationary asset. As more bitcoins are mined, the reward for mining decreases over time, a process known as halving, which occurs approximately every four years.

7. Wallets: To store and manage bitcoins, users need a digital wallet, which can be software-based (online or on a device) or hardware-based (a physical device). Wallets store the user's private keys and provide an interface to manage their Bitcoin transactions.

8. Nodes and Consensus: Nodes in the Bitcoin network validate transactions and blocks, ensuring that the rules of the protocol are followed. Consensus is achieved through a combination of cryptographic proof and economic incentives, with the majority of nodes agreeing on the state of the blockchain.

Bitcoin's operation is a blend of cryptography, game theory, and decentralized network principles, creating a secure, transparent, and resilient system for digital transactions. Understanding these mechanisms is crucial for anyone looking to invest in or use Bitcoin.

IMPORTANCE OF BITCOIN IN THE MODERN ECONOMY

Bitcoin's emergence has had significant implications for the modern economy, influencing various sectors and challenging traditional financial systems. Its importance can be understood through several key aspects:

1. Financial Inclusion: Bitcoin offers financial services to individuals who are unbanked or underbanked, particularly in regions with limited access to traditional banking infrastructure. With just a smartphone and internet connection, anyone can participate in the global economy, send and receive money, and store value securely.

2. Decentralization and Reduced Intermediaries: Bitcoin operates without central authorities or intermediaries, reducing transaction costs and increasing efficiency. This decentralization minimizes the need for traditional banks, payment processors, and other financial middlemen, allowing for faster and cheaper cross-border transactions.

3. Hedge Against Inflation: In countries experiencing hyperinflation or currency devaluation, Bitcoin serves as a store of value and a hedge against economic instability. Its limited supply and decentralized nature make it resistant to inflationary pressures, providing an alternative to fiat currencies that are subject to government policies and economic fluctuations.

4. Innovation in Financial Technology: Bitcoin has spurred significant innovation in financial technology (fintech), leading to the development of blockchain technology and a myriad of applications beyond digital currency. Blockchain's potential for secure, transparent, and efficient record-keeping is being explored in industries such as supply chain management, healthcare, and real estate.

5. Investment and Speculation: Bitcoin has become a popular asset for investors seeking high returns. Its historical price appreciation and potential for future growth have attracted both individual and institutional investors. This influx of capital and interest has led to the development of various financial products, such as Bitcoin futures and exchange-traded funds (ETFs).

6. Disruption of Traditional Financial Systems: Bitcoin challenges the traditional banking and financial systems by offering an alternative that is transparent, secure, and not controlled by any single entity. This disruption has forced financial institutions to innovate and adapt, leading to the exploration and adoption of blockchain technology in their operations.

7. Digital Gold: Often referred to as "digital gold," Bitcoin shares many properties with precious metals, such as scarcity and durability. As a result, it is increasingly viewed as a safe-haven asset, akin to gold, where investors can park their wealth during times of economic uncertainty or market volatility.

8. Empowering Individuals: Bitcoin empowers individuals by giving them greater control over their financial assets. With Bitcoin, users can manage their wealth without reliance on banks or government institutions, ensuring privacy, security, and autonomy in their financial dealings.

9. Transparency and Security: The blockchain technology underpinning Bitcoin ensures that all transactions are transparent and immutable. This transparency reduces fraud, corruption, and the need for third-party verification, enhancing trust in financial transactions and record-keeping.

10. Global Payment System: Bitcoin facilitates seamless global transactions, allowing for near-instantaneous transfers of value across borders. This capability is particularly beneficial for remittances, international trade, and online commerce, where traditional payment systems may be slow, costly, or unreliable.

Bitcoin's importance in the modern economy lies in its potential to promote financial inclusion, drive innovation, disrupt traditional financial systems, and provide a hedge against economic instability. Its impact continues to grow as adoption increases and its underlying technology evolves.

CHAPTER 2: UNDERSTANDING THE BASICS OF BITCOIN INVESTMENT

WHY INVEST IN BITCOIN?

Investing in Bitcoin has garnered significant interest over the past decade, and its potential benefits make it an attractive option for many investors. Here are key reasons to consider investing in Bitcoin:

1. High Potential for Returns: Bitcoin has demonstrated remarkable price appreciation since its inception. Early investors have seen substantial returns, and while past performance is not indicative of future results, the potential for high returns continues to attract investors seeking to capitalize on Bitcoin's growth trajectory.

2. Diversification: Bitcoin offers a unique opportunity to diversify an investment portfolio. As a non-correlated asset, Bitcoin's price movements often do not follow traditional stocks, bonds, or commodities. This diversification can help reduce overall portfolio risk and enhance returns.

3. Hedge Against Inflation: Bitcoin's fixed supply of 21 million coins makes it a deflationary asset. Unlike fiat currencies, which can be printed in unlimited quantities by central banks, Bitcoin's scarcity provides a hedge against inflation and currency devaluation, preserving purchasing power over time.

4. Decentralization and Security: Bitcoin operates on a decentralized network, reducing the risk of centralized control and censorship. Its underlying blockchain technology ensures secure and transparent transactions, making it a reliable store of value and medium of exchange.

5. Increasing Institutional Adoption: The growing acceptance of Bitcoin by institutional investors and major corporations enhances its legitimacy and potential for mainstream adoption. Companies like Tesla, Square, and MicroStrategy have made significant Bitcoin investments, while financial institutions like Fidelity and PayPal offer Bitcoin-related services, indicating broader market acceptance.

6. Digital Gold: Bitcoin is often referred to as "digital gold" due to its similar properties, such as scarcity, durability, and portability. Like gold, Bitcoin can act as a safe-haven asset during economic uncertainty, providing stability and value preservation.

7. Growing Infrastructure and Ecosystem: The Bitcoin ecosystem has matured significantly, with a robust infrastructure supporting its use and investment. Secure wallets, reputable exchanges, and regulated financial products like Bitcoin ETFs and futures contracts make it easier for investors to buy, hold, and trade Bitcoin.

8. Technological Innovation: Bitcoin's underlying blockchain technology is a revolutionary innovation with far-reaching implications. Investing in Bitcoin provides exposure to this groundbreaking technology, which is being adopted in various industries beyond finance, including supply chain management, healthcare, and real estate.

9. Global Accessibility: Bitcoin is accessible to anyone with an internet connection, making it a truly global asset. This accessibility allows investors from around the world to participate in the Bitcoin market, increasing its liquidity and potential for widespread adoption.

10. Empowerment and Financial Sovereignty: Bitcoin gives individuals control over their financial assets without relying on banks or government institutions. This financial sovereignty is particularly valuable in regions with unstable economies, restrictive financial systems, or limited access to banking services.

11. Early Adoption Advantage: While Bitcoin has grown significantly, it is still in the early stages of adoption compared to traditional financial assets. Investing in Bitcoin now offers the potential to benefit from its continued growth and adoption as the digital currency ecosystem expands.

12. Network Effects: Bitcoin benefits from network effects, where its value and utility increase as more people and institutions adopt and use it. As the network grows, Bitcoin's robustness, security, and liquidity improve, enhancing its attractiveness as an investment.

Investing in Bitcoin offers high potential returns, diversification benefits, a hedge against inflation, and exposure to innovative technology. Its growing adoption, robust infrastructure, and unique characteristics make it an appealing addition to a diversified investment portfolio. However, it's important to understand the risks involved, including volatility and regulatory uncertainty, and to approach Bitcoin investment with careful research and consideration.

RISK AND REWARD IN BITCOIN INVESTMENT

Investing in Bitcoin can be highly rewarding, but it also carries significant risks. Understanding these risks and rewards is crucial for making informed investment decisions.

REWARDS OF INVESTING IN BITCOIN

1. High Return Potential: Bitcoin has historically provided substantial returns, especially for early investors. The significant price appreciation over the past decade has attracted investors seeking high growth opportunities.

2. Portfolio Diversification: Bitcoin can diversify an investment portfolio due to its low correlation with traditional assets like stocks and bonds. This diversification can help reduce overall portfolio risk and potentially enhance returns.

3. Hedge Against Inflation: With its capped supply of 21 million coins, Bitcoin is considered a hedge against inflation. Unlike fiat currencies, which can be devalued by excessive printing, Bitcoin's scarcity helps preserve its value over time.

4. Global Accessibility: Bitcoin's decentralized nature makes it accessible to anyone with an internet connection. This global accessibility increases its liquidity and offers investment opportunities to people worldwide, including those in regions with unstable financial systems.

5. Financial Sovereignty: Bitcoin provides individuals with financial sovereignty, allowing them to control their assets without relying on banks or governments. This autonomy is particularly valuable in regions with restrictive financial regulations or economic instability.

6. Technological Innovation: Investing in Bitcoin provides exposure to the innovative blockchain technology underpinning it. Blockchain has the potential to revolutionize various industries, including finance, supply chain management, and healthcare.

RISKS OF INVESTING IN BITCOIN

1. Volatility: Bitcoin is known for its extreme price volatility. While this volatility can lead to significant gains, it can also result in substantial losses. Investors must be prepared for rapid price swings and potential market corrections.

2. Regulatory Uncertainty: The regulatory environment for Bitcoin and other cryptocurrencies is still evolving. Changes in regulations, government policies, or legal actions can impact Bitcoin's value and market dynamics. Investors should stay informed about regulatory developments and their potential effects.

3. Security Risks: Although Bitcoin transactions are secure, the ecosystem is not immune to security threats. Hacks, scams, and fraudulent exchanges can lead to loss of funds. Investors must take precautions, such as using reputable exchanges and secure wallets, to protect their investments.

4. Market Sentiment: Bitcoin's price is heavily influenced by market sentiment, news, and media coverage. Positive news can drive prices up, while negative news can lead to sharp declines. This susceptibility to sentiment makes Bitcoin a highly speculative investment.

5. Limited Adoption and Acceptance: While Bitcoin's adoption is growing, it is still not universally accepted as a medium of exchange or store of value. Limited acceptance by merchants and financial institutions can hinder its utility and long-term value.

6. Technological Risks: Bitcoin relies on complex technology, and its future depends on continued innovation and security improvements. Technical issues, such as scalability problems or vulnerabilities in the blockchain, could negatively impact its value and usability.

7. Competition from Other Cryptocurrencies: Bitcoin faces competition from other cryptocurrencies, each with unique features and use cases. Emerging technologies and projects could challenge Bitcoin's dominance and potentially reduce its market share and value.

8. Psychological Factors: Investing in Bitcoin requires managing emotional responses to market fluctuations. Fear, uncertainty, and greed can lead to poor investment decisions, such as panic selling during downturns or over-investing during bull markets.

BALANCING RISK AND REWARD

To balance the risks and rewards of Bitcoin investment:

- **Research and Education:** Understand Bitcoin, its technology, and market dynamics. Stay informed about regulatory changes and market trends.
- **Diversification:** Do not put all your investment capital into Bitcoin. Diversify your portfolio across different asset classes to mitigate risk.
- **Secure Investments:** Use reputable exchanges, secure wallets, and best practices to protect your investments from theft and fraud.
- **Risk Management:** Invest only what you can afford to lose and avoid overexposure to Bitcoin. Consider setting stop-loss orders and other risk management strategies.
- **Long-Term Perspective:** Be prepared for volatility and maintain a long-term perspective. Avoid making impulsive decisions based on short-term market movements.

By understanding the risks and rewards, and by implementing sound investment strategies, you can navigate the complexities of Bitcoin investment more effectively.

COMMON MYTHS AND MISCONCEPTIONS ABOUT BITCOIN

Bitcoin has been surrounded by numerous myths and misconceptions since its inception. Understanding the truth behind these can help investors make informed decisions and appreciate the potential of this digital currency.

1. Bitcoin is Anonymous:
Myth: Bitcoin transactions are completely anonymous, making it the perfect currency for illicit activities.

Reality: Bitcoin transactions are pseudonymous, not anonymous. While users' identities are not directly tied to their Bitcoin addresses, all transactions are recorded on the public blockchain, making them traceable. With the right tools and methods, it's possible to link transactions to individuals, which is why regulatory bodies and law enforcement can track illicit activities involving Bitcoin.

2. Bitcoin Has No Intrinsic Value:
Myth: Bitcoin is a speculative bubble with no intrinsic value, destined to collapse.

Reality: Bitcoin's value is derived from its utility, scarcity, and the trust of its users. It serves as a decentralized store of value, a medium of exchange, and a hedge against inflation. Its underlying technology, blockchain, also adds significant value by enabling secure and transparent transactions.

3. Bitcoin is Only Used for Illegal Activities:
Myth: Bitcoin is primarily used for illegal activities, such as money laundering and purchasing illegal goods.
Reality: While Bitcoin has been used for illegal activities, the majority of its transactions are legitimate. Many businesses accept Bitcoin for goods and services, and it is increasingly used for legal purposes, including remittances, investments, and charitable donations.

4. Bitcoin is a Ponzi Scheme:
Myth: Bitcoin is a Ponzi scheme designed to enrich early adopters at the expense of later investors.
Reality: Bitcoin is a decentralized digital currency with no central authority or single entity controlling it. Its value is driven by supply and demand dynamics in the market. Unlike Ponzi schemes, which rely on continuous new investment to pay returns to earlier investors, Bitcoin operates on transparent and verifiable blockchain technology.

5. Bitcoin Will Replace Traditional Currencies:

Myth: Bitcoin will completely replace traditional fiat currencies and render them obsolete.

Reality: While Bitcoin offers an alternative to fiat currencies, it is unlikely to replace them entirely. Bitcoin is more likely to coexist with traditional currencies, offering benefits such as financial inclusion, decentralized transactions, and a hedge against inflation. Governments and central banks continue to play a crucial role in the global economy.

6. Bitcoin is Too Volatile to Be a Reliable Investment:

Myth: Bitcoin's price volatility makes it an unreliable and unsafe investment.

Reality: Bitcoin is indeed volatile, but many investors consider it a high-risk, high-reward asset. Diversification and long-term investment strategies can mitigate some of the risks associated with its volatility. Over time, as adoption increases and the market matures, Bitcoin's volatility may decrease.

7. Bitcoin is Environmentally Destructive:

Myth: Bitcoin mining consumes excessive energy and is highly damaging to the environment.

Reality: Bitcoin mining does consume significant energy, but this narrative overlooks the nuances. Many miners use renewable energy sources or seek out locations with excess or cheap electricity. The industry is also exploring more energy-efficient technologies and protocols to reduce its environmental impact.

8. Bitcoin is Too Complicated for the Average Person:
Myth: Bitcoin is too complex and technical for the average person to understand or use.
Reality: While Bitcoin's underlying technology can be complex, using Bitcoin is becoming increasingly user-friendly. Many platforms, wallets, and exchanges offer intuitive interfaces and educational resources to help beginners navigate the world of Bitcoin.

9. Bitcoin is a Fad:
Myth: Bitcoin is just a passing trend that will eventually fade away.
Reality: Bitcoin has been around since 2009 and has demonstrated resilience and growth. It has gained widespread acceptance, with increasing adoption by individuals, businesses, and institutional investors. Its underlying technology,

blockchain, is also being adopted across various industries.

10. Bitcoin Transactions Are Instantaneous:
Myth: Bitcoin transactions are instantaneous.
Reality: Bitcoin transactions are not always instantaneous. While transactions are broadcast to the network quickly, they need to be confirmed by miners, which can take from a few minutes to an hour or more, depending on network congestion and transaction fees.

Addressing these myths and misconceptions helps provide a clearer understanding of Bitcoin's true nature and potential. By dispelling these misunderstandings, investors can better assess the risks and rewards associated with Bitcoin investment.

LEGAL AND REGULATORY CONSIDERATIONS

Investing in Bitcoin involves navigating a complex and evolving landscape of legal and regulatory considerations. These factors can significantly impact the value, use, and security of Bitcoin investments. Here are some key points to consider:

1. Regulatory Environment: The regulatory environment for Bitcoin varies significantly by country. Some countries have embraced Bitcoin and established clear regulatory frameworks, while others have imposed restrictions or outright bans. It's crucial for investors to understand the legal status of Bitcoin in their respective jurisdictions and stay informed about regulatory changes.

2. Taxation: Tax treatment of Bitcoin varies widely. In many countries, Bitcoin is considered property or a commodity rather than a currency. This means that capital gains tax may apply when Bitcoin is sold or exchanged. Additionally, transactions involving Bitcoin, such as purchasing goods or services, may trigger taxable events. Investors should keep detailed records of their transactions and consult with tax professionals to ensure compliance with tax laws.

3. Anti-Money Laundering (AML) and Know Your Customer (KYC) Regulations: Many countries have implemented AML and KYC regulations to prevent illegal activities such as money laundering and terrorist financing. Cryptocurrency exchanges and service providers are often required to verify the identity of their users and report suspicious activities. Investors should be prepared to provide identification and comply with these regulations when using regulated exchanges.

4. Securities Regulations: Regulators in some countries consider certain cryptocurrencies and initial coin offerings (ICOs) to be securities. If Bitcoin or related financial products (such as Bitcoin ETFs) are classified as securities, they must comply with securities laws, including registration and disclosure requirements. Investors should be aware of the regulatory status of the specific Bitcoin-related products they are investing in.

5. Consumer Protection: Consumer protection laws vary, and some jurisdictions have implemented specific regulations to protect cryptocurrency investors. These regulations may address issues such as fraud, market manipulation, and the safeguarding of customer funds. Investors should use reputable exchanges and service providers that comply with local consumer protection laws.

6. Legal Tender Status: Bitcoin is not considered legal tender in most countries, meaning it is not officially recognized as a medium of exchange for debts. However, some countries, like El Salvador, have adopted Bitcoin as legal tender, which can have significant implications for its use and acceptance.

7. Intellectual Property and Patent Issues: The technology underlying Bitcoin and other cryptocurrencies may be subject to intellectual property laws. Patents related to blockchain technology and cryptographic methods could impact the development and implementation of Bitcoin-related innovations.

8. International Considerations: For investors involved in cross-border transactions or living in multiple jurisdictions, it's essential to understand the regulatory landscape in each relevant country. Different regulatory requirements can complicate tax reporting, compliance, and legal obligations.

9. Privacy Laws: Privacy laws, such as the General Data Protection Regulation (GDPR) in the

European Union, can impact how personal data is handled by cryptocurrency exchanges and service providers. Investors should be aware of their rights under these laws and ensure that their data is protected when using cryptocurrency services.

10. Government Actions and Bans: Governments may take actions that significantly impact Bitcoin, such as implementing outright bans, restricting mining activities, or enacting strict regulatory measures. These actions can affect Bitcoin's price, liquidity, and overall market dynamics. Staying informed about potential government actions is crucial for investors.

Practical Steps for Investors:
1. Stay Informed: Regularly monitor regulatory developments in your country and globally. Join cryptocurrency forums, follow news sources, and consider consulting legal experts.

2. Choose Reputable Platforms: Use well-known and regulated exchanges and wallet providers that comply with AML, KYC, and consumer protection regulations.

3. Keep Records: Maintain detailed records of all transactions, including dates, amounts, and counterparties, for tax reporting and compliance purposes.

4. Consult Professionals: Seek advice from legal and tax professionals with expertise in cryptocurrency to navigate complex regulatory and tax issues.

5. Understand Your Rights: Be aware of your rights under privacy and consumer protection laws when using cryptocurrency services.

Navigating the legal and regulatory landscape is crucial for protecting your investment and ensuring compliance. By understanding these considerations and taking appropriate steps, investors can mitigate risks and capitalize on the opportunities presented by Bitcoin.

CHAPTER 3: SETTING UP FOR BITCOIN INVESTMENT

CHOOSING THE RIGHT BITCOIN WALLET

Choosing the right Bitcoin wallet is crucial for securely storing, managing, and transacting with your Bitcoin. There are several types of wallets, each with its own advantages and considerations. Here's a guide to help you choose the right Bitcoin wallet:

1. Types of Bitcoin Wallets:
   - **Hardware Wallets:** Hardware wallets are physical devices that store your private keys offline, providing an extra layer of security. They are considered one of the most secure options for long-term storage of large amounts of Bitcoin.

   - **Software Wallets (Desktop, Mobile, Web):** Software wallets are applications or programs that run on your desktop computer, smartphone, or web browser. They offer convenience and accessibility but may be less secure than hardware wallets, especially if the device is connected to the internet.

   - **Paper Wallets:** Paper wallets involve printing out your private keys and Bitcoin addresses on a physical piece of paper. While they are secure from online hacks, they can be vulnerable to physical damage, loss, or theft if not stored properly.

- **Multisignature Wallets:** Multisignature wallets require multiple private keys to authorize transactions, adding an extra layer of security. They are commonly used by businesses and organizations to manage funds securely.

2. Key Considerations:
- **Security:** Consider the security features of the wallet, such as encryption, backup options, and whether it supports multisignature transactions.

- **Convenience:** Evaluate the user interface and ease of use of the wallet. Choose a wallet that suits your technical proficiency and preferences.

- **Compatibility:** Ensure that the wallet is compatible with your device and operating system. Check whether it supports the features you need, such as multi-currency support or integration with hardware wallets.

- **Privacy:** Look for wallets that prioritize user privacy and offer features such as coin control, Tor integration, or support for privacy-focused cryptocurrencies like Monero.

- **Reputation:** Choose wallets developed by reputable companies or open-source projects with a track record of security and reliability. Check reviews and feedback from other users to assess the wallet's reputation.

- **Customer Support:** Consider the level of customer support offered by the wallet provider. Look for wallets with responsive customer service channels in case you encounter any issues or need assistance.

3. **Recommended Wallets:**
   - **Hardware Wallets:** Ledger Nano S, Ledger Nano X, Trezor Model T
   - **Software Wallets:** Electrum (Desktop), Trust Wallet (Mobile), MyEtherWallet (Web)
   - **Multisignature Wallets:** Casa, Electrum (supports multisig functionality)

4. **Additional Tips:**
   - **Backup Your Wallet:** Always backup your wallet's seed phrase or private keys in a secure location. This ensures that you can recover your

funds in case your device is lost, stolen, or damaged.

- **Update Regularly:** Keep your wallet software up to date with the latest security patches and features. Updates often include bug fixes and improvements to enhance security and usability.

- **Practice Safe Storage:** If using a hardware wallet, store it in a secure location, such as a safe or safety deposit box. Avoid sharing your private keys or seed phrases with anyone and be cautious of phishing attempts or scams.

Choosing the right Bitcoin wallet requires careful consideration of security, convenience, compatibility, and reputation. By evaluating these factors and following best practices for wallet security, you can confidently store and manage your Bitcoin holdings.

SETTING UP A SECURE WALLET

Setting up a secure wallet is essential for safeguarding your Bitcoin holdings from theft, loss, and unauthorized access. Here's a step-by-step guide to help you set up a secure Bitcoin wallet:

1. Choose a Secure Wallet:
   - Select a reputable and secure wallet provider that offers features like encryption, backup options, and multisignature support.
   - Consider factors such as the type of wallet (hardware, software, paper), security features, compatibility, and reputation.

2. Download or Purchase the Wallet:
   - If you're using a software wallet, download the official wallet application from the provider's website or app store.
   - If you're using a hardware wallet, purchase the device from an authorized retailer or the manufacturer's website.

3. Follow Installation Instructions:
   - Install the wallet software on your device following the instructions provided by the wallet provider.

- For hardware wallets, follow the setup instructions included in the packaging or provided by the manufacturer.

4. Set Up a Strong Password:
- Create a strong and unique password for your wallet. Use a combination of uppercase and lowercase letters, numbers, and special characters.
- Avoid using easily guessable passwords or reusing passwords from other accounts.

5. Backup Your Wallet:
- Most wallets will provide you with a recovery seed phrase or mnemonic phrase during setup. Write down this seed phrase and store it in a safe and secure location, such as a physical safe or safety deposit box.
- Do not store the seed phrase digitally or share it with anyone else. It is the key to accessing your wallet and should be kept confidential.

6. Enable Two-Factor Authentication (2FA):
- If your wallet supports two-factor authentication (2FA), enable this feature for an extra layer of security. This typically involves linking your wallet to a mobile authenticator app or receiving SMS codes for account verification.

- Two-factor authentication helps prevent unauthorized access to your wallet, even if someone obtains your password.

7. Test Your Wallet:
- Send a small amount of Bitcoin to your wallet to test its functionality. Ensure that you can send and receive transactions correctly and access your funds using your password and recovery seed.

8. Keep Your Software Updated:
- Regularly update your wallet software to the latest version to ensure you have the latest security patches and features.
- Pay attention to security alerts or notifications from the wallet provider and take action promptly if any vulnerabilities are identified.

9. Practice Safe Usage:
- Avoid accessing your wallet on public or unsecured networks. Use a secure and trusted internet connection when interacting with your wallet.
- Be cautious of phishing attempts, scams, and malware that may attempt to steal your login credentials or seed phrase.

- Never share your password or recovery seed with anyone, and be wary of unsolicited messages or requests for sensitive information.

10. Regularly Backup Your Wallet:
- Periodically backup your wallet, especially after making significant changes or transactions. Update your backup seed phrase if necessary and ensure it remains secure.

By following these steps and best practices, you can set up a secure Bitcoin wallet and protect your digital assets from potential threats and vulnerabilities.

UNDERSTANDING BITCOIN EXCHANGES

Understanding Bitcoin exchanges is crucial for buying, selling, and trading Bitcoin. Bitcoin exchanges are platforms that facilitate the exchange of Bitcoin for fiat currency (such as USD, EUR, etc.) or other cryptocurrencies. Here's a comprehensive guide to help you understand Bitcoin exchanges:

1. Types of Bitcoin Exchanges:
   - **Centralized Exchanges (CEX):** Centralized exchanges operate as intermediaries between buyers and sellers, matching orders and facilitating trades. They typically require users to create accounts, undergo identity verification (KYC), and deposit funds before trading. Examples include Coinbase, Binance, and Kraken.

   - **Decentralized Exchanges (DEX):** Decentralized exchanges operate on blockchain networks and allow users to trade directly with one another without the need for intermediaries. They offer greater privacy and security, as users retain control of their funds and identities. Examples include Uniswap, SushiSwap, and PancakeSwap.

   - **Peer-to-Peer (P2P) Exchanges:** Peer-to-peer exchanges connect buyers and sellers directly, allowing them to negotiate prices and terms of trade. P2P exchanges provide more privacy and flexibility but require users to conduct due diligence and verify the counterparty's trustworthiness. Examples include LocalBitcoins and Paxful.

2. Key Features of Bitcoin Exchanges:
   - **Trading Pairs:** Bitcoin exchanges offer various trading pairs, allowing users to trade Bitcoin for fiat currency (e.g., BTC/USD) or other cryptocurrencies (e.g., BTC/ETH).

   - **Order Types:** Exchanges support different types of orders, including market orders, limit orders, and stop-loss orders, allowing users to execute trades at specific prices or conditions.

   - **Liquidity:** Liquidity refers to the ease with which assets can be bought or sold on an exchange. Exchanges with higher liquidity tend to have tighter bid-ask spreads and lower slippage.

   - **Fees:** Exchanges charge fees for trading, depositing, withdrawing, and other services. Fees vary by exchange and can include maker/taker fees, trading fees, withdrawal fees, and network fees.

   - **Security:** Security is paramount when choosing an exchange. Look for exchanges that implement industry best practices for security, such as cold storage of funds, two-factor authentication (2FA), and regular security audits.

3. Factors to Consider When Choosing an Exchange:

- **Security:** Prioritize exchanges with a strong track record of security and a commitment to protecting user funds and data.

- **Regulation:** Consider whether the exchange is regulated in its jurisdiction and compliant with relevant laws and regulations, especially if you prioritize investor protection and regulatory compliance.

- **User Experience:** Choose exchanges with intuitive user interfaces, responsive customer support, and reliable trading infrastructure to ensure a seamless trading experience.

- **Liquidity:** Opt for exchanges with sufficient liquidity to ensure efficient order execution and minimize slippage.

- **Fees:** Compare fee structures across different exchanges and consider the impact of fees on your trading activity, especially if you plan to trade frequently or in large volumes.

4. Tips for Using Bitcoin Exchanges:
   - **Start with Small Trades:** If you're new to trading, start with small trades to familiarize yourself with the platform's features and assess its performance.

   - **Secure Your Account:** Enable two-factor authentication (2FA), use strong and unique passwords, and be cautious of phishing attempts or suspicious activity on your account.

   - **Do Your Research:** Conduct thorough research on exchanges before depositing funds or trading. Read reviews, check community forums, and verify the exchange's reputation and reliability.

   - **Withdraw Funds Securely:** Store your funds securely in a personal wallet rather than leaving them on the exchange, especially if you're holding large amounts of Bitcoin.

Understanding Bitcoin exchanges and choosing the right one for your needs is essential for safely and efficiently participating in the cryptocurrency market. By considering factors such as security, regulation, liquidity, and fees, you can select an exchange that aligns with your trading goals and preferences.

STEPS TO BUYING YOUR FIRST BITCOIN

Buying your first Bitcoin can be an exciting and rewarding experience. Here's a step-by-step guide to help you navigate the process:

1. Choose a Bitcoin Wallet: Before buying Bitcoin, you'll need a secure wallet to store your digital assets. Consider factors such as security features, convenience, and compatibility when selecting a wallet. Popular options include hardware wallets like Ledger Nano S or software wallets like Electrum.

2. Select a Reputable Bitcoin Exchange: Choose a reputable and trustworthy Bitcoin exchange where you can buy Bitcoin with fiat currency (e.g., USD, EUR) or other cryptocurrencies. Look for exchanges with a strong track record of security, regulatory compliance, and positive user reviews. Some popular exchanges include Coinbase, Binance, and Kraken.

3. Sign Up and Verify Your Account: Sign up for an account on your chosen Bitcoin exchange and complete the verification process. This typically involves providing personal information, such as your name, address, and photo ID, to comply with Know Your Customer (KYC) and Anti-Money Laundering (AML) regulations.

4. Deposit Funds into Your Exchange Account: Once your account is verified, deposit funds into your exchange account using a bank transfer, credit/debit card, or other supported payment methods. Follow the instructions provided by the exchange to complete the deposit process.

5. Place an Order to Buy Bitcoin: Navigate to the trading section of the exchange and place an order to buy Bitcoin. Choose the amount of Bitcoin you want to purchase and specify the price at which you're willing to buy. You can place a market order to buy Bitcoin at the current market price or a limit order to specify a price you're willing to pay.

6. Monitor Your Order and Confirm Purchase: Once you've placed your order, monitor its status on the exchange's trading platform. If you placed a market order, your purchase will be executed immediately at the current market price.

If you placed a limit order, your purchase will be executed when the market reaches your specified price.

Once your order is filled, you'll receive a confirmation notification from the exchange, and your Bitcoin will be credited to your exchange account.

7. Transfer Bitcoin to Your Wallet: For enhanced security, consider transferring your purchased Bitcoin from the exchange to your personal wallet. Locate the withdrawal option on the exchange and enter your wallet address to initiate the transfer. Double-check the address to ensure accuracy, as transactions cannot be reversed once initiated.

8. Securely Store Your Bitcoin: After transferring your Bitcoin to your personal wallet, securely store your wallet's private keys or recovery seed phrase in a safe and confidential location. This ensures that you have access to your Bitcoin in case of loss, theft, or device failure.

9. Stay Informed and Practice Safe Trading: Stay informed about market trends, news, and developments in the cryptocurrency space to make informed trading decisions. Practice safe trading practices, such as using secure passwords, enabling two-factor authentication (2FA), and avoiding phishing scams.

By following these steps and exercising caution, you can safely and confidently buy your first Bitcoin and embark on your journey into the world of cryptocurrency investing.

CHAPTER 4: DEVELOPING YOUR INVESTMENT STRATEGY

DEFINING YOUR INVESTMENT GOALS

Defining your investment goals is a crucial first step before diving into Bitcoin or any other investment. Here's a guide to help you clarify your investment objectives:

1. Determine Your Time Horizon: Consider your investment timeframe, whether it's short-term, medium-term, or long-term. Short-term goals may include generating quick profits, while long-term goals may focus on wealth accumulation or retirement planning.

2. Assess Your Risk Tolerance: Evaluate your risk tolerance and willingness to withstand market volatility and potential losses. Consider factors such as your financial situation, investment experience, and comfort level with risk.

3. Define Your Financial Objectives: Clearly outline your financial objectives and what you hope to achieve through your investments. This could include goals such as:
   - Building wealth and financial security

- Generating passive income
- Saving for a specific milestone (e.g., buying a house, funding education)
- Preserving capital and protecting against inflation

4. Consider Your Investment Strategy: Determine your investment strategy based on your goals, risk tolerance, and market outlook. This could involve:

- **Dollar-cost averaging:** Investing a fixed amount of money at regular intervals to smooth out market fluctuations.
- **Value investing:** Seeking undervalued assets with long-term growth potential.
- **Growth investing:** Investing in high-growth assets with the potential for significant returns.
- **Diversification:** Spreading your investments across different asset classes to reduce risk.
- **Hedging:** Using strategies to offset potential losses or protect against downside risk.

5. Set Clear, Measurable Goals:
- Set clear and measurable investment goals that are specific, achievable, relevant, and time-bound (SMART goals). For example:
- "I want to achieve a 10% annual return on my investment portfolio over the next five years."

- "I aim to accumulate $100,000 in savings for retirement by age 40."

- "I plan to generate $500 per month in passive income from my investments within two years."

6. Review and Adjust Your Goals Regularly: Regularly review your investment goals and portfolio performance to ensure they align with your evolving financial situation, market conditions, and personal priorities. Be prepared to adjust your goals and investment strategy as needed.

7. Consider Tax Implications: Take into account the tax implications of your investment decisions, including capital gains taxes, income taxes, and potential deductions or credits. Consult with a tax advisor to optimize your tax strategy and minimize tax liabilities.

8. Seek Professional Advice if Needed: If you're unsure about setting investment goals or developing a suitable strategy, consider seeking advice from a financial advisor or investment professional. They can provide personalized guidance based on your individual circumstances and help you make informed decisions.

By defining your investment goals and objectives upfront, you can establish a clear roadmap for your investment journey, make more informed decisions, and work towards achieving your financial aspirations.

LONG-TERM VS. SHORT-TERM INVESTMENT

Differentiating between long-term and short-term investments is essential for aligning your investment strategy with your financial goals and risk tolerance. Here's a comparison of long-term and short-term investments to help you make informed decisions:

1. Time Horizon:
  - Short-Term Investments:
    - Typically held for a period of one year or less.
    - Suited for investors with immediate liquidity needs or those looking to capitalize on short-term market opportunities.

  - Long-Term Investments:
    - Held for an extended period, usually several years or more.

- Designed to accumulate wealth over time and achieve long-term financial objectives, such as retirement planning or wealth preservation.

2. Risk and Return:
- Short-Term Investments:
- Tend to be less volatile but offer lower potential returns compared to long-term investments.
- Examples include cash equivalents, certificates of deposit (CDs), short-term bonds, and money market funds.

- Long-Term Investments:
- Generally have higher volatility but offer the potential for greater returns over an extended period.
- Examples include stocks, real estate, long-term bonds, and equity mutual funds.

3. Investment Goals:
- Short-Term Investments:
- Suited for achieving immediate financial goals or preserving capital in the short term.
- Used for purposes such as building an emergency fund, saving for a vacation, or making a down payment on a home.

- Long-Term Investments:
- Geared towards achieving long-term financial objectives, such as retirement planning, wealth accumulation, or funding education expenses.
- Provide the opportunity for compound growth over time, as investment returns are reinvested and accumulate.

4. Liquidity:
- Short-Term Investments:
- Offer high liquidity, meaning they can be easily converted into cash without significant loss of value.
- Investors can access their funds quickly and with minimal transaction costs.

- Long-Term Investments:
- Often have lower liquidity, as they require a longer time horizon to realize their full potential returns.
- Selling long-term investments may involve transaction fees, market volatility, and potential tax implications.

5. Tax Implications:
- Short-Term Investments:
- Gains from short-term investments are typically taxed at higher ordinary income tax rates.

- Investors may incur capital gains taxes if they sell short-term investments at a profit within one year of purchase.

- Long-Term Investments:
- Gains from long-term investments are generally taxed at lower capital gains tax rates.
- Investors may qualify for preferential tax treatment, such as the long-term capital gains tax rate, if they hold investments for more than one year.

6. Diversification:
- Short-Term Investments:
- Offer limited opportunities for diversification, as they are often limited to low-risk, low-return assets.
- Investors may need to accept lower returns in exchange for greater stability and liquidity.

- Long-Term Investments:
- Provide greater opportunities for diversification across asset classes, sectors, and geographic regions.
- Diversification can help mitigate risk and enhance overall portfolio performance over the long term.

7. Monitoring and Adjustments:
- Short-Term Investments:
- Require more frequent monitoring and adjustments to capitalize on short-term market movements or changes in financial conditions.
- Investors may need to rebalance their portfolio or reallocate funds periodically to maintain their desired asset allocation.

- Long-Term Investments:
- Generally require less frequent monitoring and adjustments, as they are based on a buy-and-hold strategy.
- Investors should periodically review their long-term investment portfolio and make adjustments based on changes in their financial goals, risk tolerance, or market conditions.

Choosing between long-term and short-term investments depends on your individual financial goals, risk tolerance, and time horizon. By understanding the characteristics and considerations of each investment horizon, you can develop a well-rounded investment strategy that aligns with your objectives and maximizes your potential for financial success.

DIVERSIFYING YOUR BITCOIN PORTFOLIO

Diversifying your Bitcoin portfolio is a prudent strategy to manage risk and maximize potential returns. Here's a guide to help you diversify your Bitcoin holdings effectively:

1. Understand Diversification: Diversification involves spreading your investments across different assets, sectors, and geographic regions to reduce the impact of any single investment's performance on your overall portfolio.

2. Consider Alternative Cryptocurrencies (Altcoins): Bitcoin is the most well-known cryptocurrency, but there are thousands of other cryptocurrencies (altcoins) with unique features and use cases. Consider allocating a portion of your portfolio to select altcoins with promising technology, strong development teams, and active communities.

3. Invest in Non-Cryptocurrency Assets: Diversify your portfolio by investing in non-cryptocurrency assets such as stocks, bonds, real estate, commodities, and precious metals. These traditional assets can provide stability and diversification benefits to your overall investment portfolio.

4. Allocate Across Different Investment Strategies:
   - Allocate your Bitcoin holdings across different investment strategies, such as:
      - **Long-term holding:** Hold a portion of your Bitcoin as a long-term investment, taking advantage of its potential for capital appreciation over time.
      - **Trading:** Allocate a smaller portion of your portfolio for short-term trading or speculation on Bitcoin price movements.
      - **Staking or lending:** Participate in staking or lending programs to earn additional income on your Bitcoin holdings.

5. Utilize Dollar-Cost Averaging (DCA):
   - Implement a dollar-cost averaging (DCA) strategy to gradually accumulate Bitcoin over time by investing a fixed amount of money at regular intervals (e.g., weekly or monthly). DCA can help smooth out market volatility and reduce the risk of buying at a single high price point.

6. Manage Risk with Position Sizing: Determine the appropriate allocation size for each asset in your portfolio based on your risk tolerance, investment objectives, and market conditions. Avoid overexposure to any single asset class or investment strategy.

7. Rebalance Your Portfolio Regularly: Periodically review and rebalance your portfolio to maintain your desired asset allocation and risk profile. Rebalancing involves selling assets that have appreciated in value and reinvesting the proceeds into underperforming assets to restore the original asset allocation.

8. Stay Informed and Adapt: Stay informed about market trends, news, and developments in the cryptocurrency space and broader financial markets. Be prepared to adapt your investment strategy based on changing market conditions, regulatory developments, and macroeconomic factors.

9. Secure Your Investments: Ensure that your investments are securely stored in reputable wallets or custody solutions that prioritize security and protect against theft, hacking, or loss.

10. Seek Professional Advice if Needed: If you're unsure about how to diversify your Bitcoin portfolio or develop a suitable investment strategy, consider seeking advice from a financial advisor or investment professional with expertise in cryptocurrencies and portfolio management.

Diversifying your Bitcoin portfolio can help mitigate risk, enhance long-term returns, and improve overall portfolio resilience. By allocating your investments across different assets, strategies, and investment horizons, you can build a well-rounded portfolio that aligns with your financial goals and risk tolerance.

MANAGING RISKS AND VOLATILITY

Managing risks and volatility is essential when investing in Bitcoin or any other asset class. Here are some strategies to help you navigate the risks associated with Bitcoin investment:

1. Diversification: Diversify your investment portfolio across different asset classes, such as stocks, bonds, real estate, and cryptocurrencies. Diversification can help reduce the impact of any single asset's volatility on your overall portfolio.

2. Dollar-Cost Averaging (DCA): Implement a dollar-cost averaging strategy by investing a fixed amount of money into Bitcoin at regular intervals, regardless of market conditions. DCA can help mitigate the risk of investing a large sum at a single high price point and smooth out the impact of market volatility over time.

3. Set Realistic Expectations: Understand that Bitcoin is a highly volatile asset and be prepared for price fluctuations. Set realistic investment goals and expectations based on historical price trends and market dynamics.

4. Risk Assessment and Management: Assess your risk tolerance and investment objectives before investing in Bitcoin. Only invest what you can afford to lose and avoid taking excessive risks that could jeopardize your financial stability.

5. Use Stop-Loss Orders: Consider using stop-loss orders to automatically sell your Bitcoin if its price falls below a predetermined level. Stop-loss orders can help limit potential losses and protect your investment capital during periods of market downturns.

6. Stay Informed and Educated: Stay informed about market trends, news, and developments in the cryptocurrency space. Educate yourself about Bitcoin fundamentals, technology, and market dynamics to make informed investment decisions.

7. Avoid Emotional Decision-Making: Avoid making impulsive decisions based on emotions such as fear or greed. Stick to your investment plan and avoid reacting to short-term price fluctuations or market noise.

8. Secure Your Investments: Use reputable and secure wallets or custody solutions to store your Bitcoin holdings. Implement best practices for securing your digital assets, such as using hardware wallets, enabling two-factor authentication (2FA), and keeping your private keys offline.

9. Consider Hedging Strategies: Explore hedging strategies such as options, futures contracts, or derivatives to mitigate downside risk and protect against adverse price movements. Hedging can help offset potential losses and provide downside protection in volatile markets.

10. Stay Patient and Disciplined: Remain patient and disciplined during periods of market volatility. Avoid succumbing to panic selling or FOMO (fear of missing out) and stick to your long-term investment plan.

By implementing these risk management strategies and staying disciplined in your investment approach, you can better manage the risks and volatility associated with Bitcoin investment and position yourself for long-term success in the cryptocurrency market.

CHAPTER 5: ANALYZING THE MARKET

READING BITCOIN CHARTS

Reading Bitcoin charts is essential for understanding price movements, identifying trends, and making informed investment decisions. Here's a guide to help you interpret Bitcoin charts effectively:

1. Choose a Charting Platform: Select a reliable charting platform that provides real-time or historical price data for Bitcoin. Popular charting platforms include TradingView, CoinGecko, CoinMarketCap, and CryptoCompare.

2. Understand Chart Types: Familiarize yourself with different types of charts commonly used in technical analysis, including:
 - **Line Chart:** Displays the closing prices of Bitcoin over a specified time period, plotted as a continuous line.
 - **Candlestick Chart:** Provides more detailed information, including opening, closing, high, and low prices for each time period (e.g., hourly, daily). Candlestick charts are visually represented as

"candles," with different colors indicating bullish (green) and bearish (red) price movements.

   - **Bar Chart:** Similar to candlestick charts but represented as vertical bars, with the top and bottom of each bar representing the high and low prices, respectively.

3. Analyze Price Trends: Identify key price trends and patterns on the Bitcoin chart, such as:

   - **Trendlines:** Draw trendlines to connect consecutive highs or lows to identify upward or downward trends.

   - **Support and Resistance Levels:** Identify significant support (price floor) and resistance (price ceiling) levels where price tends to react or reverse.

   - **Moving Averages:** Use moving averages (e.g., 50-day, 200-day) to smooth out price fluctuations and identify trend direction. Golden cross (short-term moving average crossing above long-term moving average) and death cross (short-term moving average crossing below long-term moving average) are common bullish and bearish signals, respectively.

4. Utilize Technical Indicators: Apply technical indicators to analyze price momentum, volatility, and strength, such as:

- **Relative Strength Index (RSI):** Measures the magnitude of recent price changes to assess overbought (above 70) or oversold (below 30) conditions.

- **Moving Average Convergence Divergence (MACD):** Provides signals based on the convergence or divergence of two moving averages to identify trend reversals or momentum shifts.

- **Bollinger Bands:** Consist of a moving average and upper/lower bands representing standard deviations from the moving average, used to gauge volatility and potential price reversals.

5. Monitor Volume: Pay attention to trading volume (the number of Bitcoin units traded over a specified time period) to confirm price movements and identify potential trend reversals. High volume during price rallies or sell-offs can indicate market strength or weakness, respectively.

6. Combine Multiple Timeframes: Analyze Bitcoin charts across multiple timeframes (e.g., hourly, daily, weekly) to gain a comprehensive view of price trends and patterns. Longer time frames provide broader perspective, while shorter timeframes offer more detailed insights into intraday price movements.

7. Conduct Fundamental Analysis: Supplement technical analysis with fundamental analysis by considering factors such as market sentiment, macroeconomic trends, regulatory developments, and adoption metrics. Fundamental analysis can provide context and validate technical signals.

8. Practice and Gain Experience: Practice reading Bitcoin charts regularly and gain experience by observing price movements and analyzing historical data. Develop your charting skills over time and refine your trading strategy based on observation and analysis.

By mastering the art of reading Bitcoin charts, you can gain valuable insights into market dynamics, anticipate price movements, and make informed trading decisions in the cryptocurrency market.

TECHNICAL ANALYSIS BASICS

Technical analysis is a method of analyzing financial markets and forecasting price movements based on historical price data and trading volume. Here are the basics of technical analysis:

1. Price Charts: Price charts are graphical representations of historical price data for a particular asset, such as stocks, currencies, or cryptocurrencies like Bitcoin. Common types of charts used in technical analysis include line charts, bar charts, and candlestick charts.

2. Support and Resistance Levels: Support levels are price levels at which a security tends to find buying interest and bounce higher, preventing further price declines. Resistance levels are price levels at which a security tends to encounter selling pressure and struggle to move higher. Identifying support and resistance levels helps traders anticipate potential price reversals.

3. Trend Analysis: Trends are directional movements in price that persist over time. Technical analysts use trend analysis to identify the direction of the prevailing trend (upward, downward, or sideways) and to anticipate potential trend reversals. Common tools for trend analysis include trendlines, moving averages, and trend indicators.

4. Chart Patterns: Chart patterns are recurring formations or structures on price charts that provide clues about future price movements. Common chart patterns include:

- **Head and Shoulders:** A reversal pattern characterized by three peaks, with the middle peak (head) higher than the two surrounding peaks (shoulders).

- **Double Top and Double Bottom:** Reversal patterns marked by two consecutive peaks (double top) or troughs (double bottom) at similar price levels.

- **Symmetrical Triangle, Ascending Triangle, and Descending Triangle:** Continuation patterns formed by converging trendlines, indicating a period of consolidation before the resumption of the prevailing trend.

5. Technical Indicators:

- Technical indicators are mathematical calculations based on price and volume data that help traders analyze market trends, momentum, and volatility. Common technical indicators include:

- **Moving Averages:** Smoothed averages of past price data that help identify trend direction and potential support/resistance levels.
   - **Relative Strength Index (RSI):** A momentum oscillator that measures the speed and change of price movements, indicating overbought (above 70) or oversold (below 30) conditions.
   - **MACD (Moving Average Convergence Divergence):** A trend-following momentum indicator that shows the relationship between two moving averages of an asset's price.

6. **Volume Analysis:** Volume is the number of shares or units of a security traded during a given period. Volume analysis helps confirm price trends and signals, as changes in trading volume often precede price movements. Increasing volume during price rallies or sell-offs can confirm the strength of a trend, while declining volume may indicate weakening momentum.

7. **Risk Management:** Risk management is essential in technical analysis to protect capital and minimize losses. Traders use risk management techniques such as setting stop-loss orders, position sizing, and diversification to manage risk effectively and preserve trading capital.

8. Limitations of Technical Analysis: Technical analysis has limitations, including the subjective nature of interpreting chart patterns and indicators, the inability to predict unforeseen events or fundamental factors that may impact prices, and the risk of false signals or noise in price data.

By mastering the basics of technical analysis, traders can gain valuable insights into market trends, identify trading opportunities, and make informed decisions about buying, selling, or holding assets. However, it's essential to complement technical analysis with fundamental analysis and risk management techniques for a comprehensive approach to trading and investing.

FUNDAMENTAL ANALYSIS OF BITCOIN

Fundamental analysis of Bitcoin involves evaluating factors that influence its intrinsic value, adoption, and long-term viability as a digital currency and store of value. Here's how you can conduct fundamental analysis of Bitcoin:

1. Network Metrics:
Assess network metrics such as:

- **Hash Rate:** The computing power dedicated to mining Bitcoin blocks, which reflects the security and resilience of the Bitcoin network.

- **Difficulty Adjustment:** The rate at which the mining difficulty adjusts to maintain a consistent block production interval, indicating network health and stability.

- **Transaction Volume:** The number and value of transactions processed on the Bitcoin network, reflecting user adoption and network activity.

2. Adoption and Usage:
Analyze Bitcoin's adoption and usage metrics, including:

- **Number of Wallets:** The number of active Bitcoin wallets and addresses, indicating user adoption and network growth.

- **Merchant Adoption:** The number of merchants and businesses accepting Bitcoin as payment, which reflects its utility as a medium of exchange.

- **Transaction Fees:** The average transaction fees paid to miners for processing Bitcoin transactions, reflecting network congestion and demand for block space.

3. Regulatory Environment: Monitor regulatory developments and government policies related to Bitcoin and cryptocurrencies. Regulatory clarity and favorable regulations can enhance investor confidence and facilitate mainstream adoption, while regulatory uncertainty may impact Bitcoin's price and adoption negatively.

4. Market Sentiment: Gauge market sentiment and investor confidence through sentiment analysis, social media activity, news sentiment, and surveys. Positive sentiment and growing interest in Bitcoin may drive prices higher, while negative sentiment or fear may lead to selling pressure and price declines.

5. Institutional Adoption:
Track institutional adoption and investment in Bitcoin, including:
  - **Institutional Investors:** The participation of institutional investors, hedge funds, and corporations in Bitcoin investment and custody services.
  - **Bitcoin Investment Products:** The launch of Bitcoin exchange-traded funds (ETFs), futures contracts, and other investment products aimed at institutional investors.
  - **Corporate Treasury Reserves:** The allocation of Bitcoin reserves by publicly traded companies as part of their corporate treasury

strategy, indicating growing acceptance of Bitcoin as a store of value.

6. Technological Developments:
Stay informed about technological developments and innovations in the Bitcoin ecosystem, such as:

   - **Layer 2 Solutions:** Scaling solutions like the Lightning Network, which enable faster and cheaper Bitcoin transactions off-chain.

   - **Privacy Enhancements:** Improvements to Bitcoin's privacy features and protocols, enhancing fungibility and transaction anonymity.

   - **Smart Contract Functionality:** Integration of smart contract capabilities on Bitcoin through sidechains or second-layer solutions, expanding its use cases beyond simple value transfer.

7. Economic Factors: Consider broader economic factors and macroeconomic trends that may impact Bitcoin's price and adoption, such as:

   - **Monetary Policy:** Central bank actions, inflation rates, and currency debasement concerns that may drive demand for non-inflationary assets like Bitcoin.

   - **Geopolitical Tensions:** Political instability, trade conflicts, and geopolitical tensions that may increase demand for Bitcoin as a hedge against systemic risks and currency devaluation.

By conducting fundamental analysis of Bitcoin, investors can gain insights into its underlying value proposition, adoption trends, and long-term prospects. However, it's essential to complement fundamental analysis with technical analysis, risk management, and a thorough understanding of market dynamics for a well-rounded investment approach.

STAYING INFORMED WITH NEWS AND TRENDS

Staying informed about news and trends is crucial for making informed decisions when investing in Bitcoin. Here's how you can stay up-to-date with the latest developments:

1. Follow Cryptocurrency News Outlets: Stay informed by regularly reading news websites, blogs, and forums dedicated to cryptocurrencies and Bitcoin. Some popular cryptocurrency news outlets include CoinDesk, CoinTelegraph, CryptoSlate, and Decrypt.

2. Monitor Social Media Channels: Follow influential figures, industry experts, and cryptocurrency influencers on social media platforms like Twitter, Reddit, and LinkedIn. Engage in discussions, share insights, and stay updated with real-time news and market commentary.

3. Join Online Communities: Participate in online communities and forums dedicated to Bitcoin and cryptocurrencies, such as Reddit's r/Bitcoin and BitcoinTalk.org. Engage with fellow enthusiasts, ask questions, share knowledge, and stay updated with community-driven news and discussions.

4. Subscribe to Newsletters and Podcasts: Subscribe to newsletters, podcasts, and YouTube channels that cover Bitcoin and cryptocurrency-related topics. These platforms provide valuable insights, analysis, and interviews with industry experts, thought leaders, and insiders.

5. Follow Official Announcements: Keep track of official announcements, updates, and releases from Bitcoin developers, core contributors, and key stakeholders. Follow Bitcoin's official website, GitHub repositories, and social media channels for the latest project developments and protocol upgrades.

6. Set Up Price Alerts: Use cryptocurrency price tracking apps or platforms to set up price alerts for Bitcoin. Receive notifications when Bitcoin's price reaches predefined levels, allowing you to stay informed and react promptly to market movements.

7. Attend Events and Conferences: Attend cryptocurrency conferences, meetups, and events to network with industry professionals, learn about the latest trends and developments, and gain valuable insights from keynote speakers and panel discussions.

8. Read White papers and Research Reports: Dive deeper into Bitcoin's technology, economics, and fundamentals by reading whitepapers, research reports, and academic papers. Stay informed about new research findings, technical advancements, and emerging trends shaping the future of Bitcoin.

9. Stay Informed About Regulatory Developments: Keep track of regulatory developments and government policies related to Bitcoin and cryptocurrencies. Monitor legislative proposals, regulatory guidance, and enforcement actions that may impact Bitcoin's legal status, adoption, and market sentiment.

10. Use Aggregator Platforms: Utilize aggregator platforms and news aggregators that curate news and updates from multiple sources. Platforms like Google News, Flipboard, and Feedly allow you to customize your news feed and stay updated with the latest headlines and trends.

Staying informed about news and trends, you can make more informed decisions, anticipate market movements, and navigate the dynamic landscape of Bitcoin and cryptocurrency investing with greater confidence.

CHAPTER 6: BEST PRACTICES AND FUTURE TRENDS

BEST PRACTICES FOR SAFE INVESTING

Safe investing involves minimizing risks and protecting your capital while seeking returns. Here are some best practices for safe investing in Bitcoin:

1. Conduct Research: Educate yourself about Bitcoin and cryptocurrencies before investing. Understand the technology, market dynamics, and potential risks associated with investing in Bitcoin.

2. Start Small: Start with a small investment amount that you can afford to lose. Avoid investing more than you can afford to lose, especially if you're new to Bitcoin or cryptocurrencies.

3. Diversify Your Portfolio: Diversify your investment portfolio across different asset classes, sectors, and geographic regions to reduce risk. Don't put all your eggs in one basket, and consider allocating only a portion of your portfolio to Bitcoin and cryptocurrencies.

4. Invest for the Long Term: Take a long-term perspective when investing in Bitcoin. Avoid making impulsive decisions based on short-term price fluctuations, and focus on the fundamentals and long-term potential of Bitcoin as a digital store of value.

5. Use Dollar-Cost Averaging (DCA): Implement a dollar-cost averaging strategy by investing a fixed amount of money into Bitcoin at regular intervals (e.g., weekly or monthly). DCA can help smooth out market volatility and reduce the risk of buying at a single high price point.

6. Set Realistic Goals: Set realistic investment goals and expectations based on your financial situation, risk tolerance, and investment horizon. Avoid chasing unrealistic returns or speculative investments that promise quick profits.

7. Practice Risk Management: Manage risk by setting stop-loss orders, diversifying your investments, and avoiding excessive leverage. Only invest what you can afford to lose, and don't risk more than you're willing to lose.

8. Secure Your Investments: Use reputable and secure wallets or custody solutions to store your

Bitcoin holdings. Implement best practices for securing your digital assets, such as using hardware wallets, enabling two-factor authentication (2FA), and keeping your private keys offline.

9. Stay Informed: Stay informed about news, trends, and developments in the Bitcoin and cryptocurrency space. Keep track of regulatory developments, market sentiment, and technological advancements that may impact Bitcoin's price and adoption.

10. Seek Professional Advice: Consider seeking advice from a financial advisor or investment professional with expertise in cryptocurrencies and portfolio management. A professional can provide personalized guidance based on your individual circumstances and help you make informed investment decisions.

By following these best practices for safe investing, you can minimize risks, protect your capital, and navigate the dynamic landscape of Bitcoin and cryptocurrency investing with greater confidence and peace of mind.

COMMON MISTAKES TO AVOID

When investing in Bitcoin, it's crucial to avoid common mistakes that can jeopardize your investment goals and financial security. Here are some mistakes to avoid:

1. Investing Without Research: One of the most common mistakes is investing in Bitcoin without understanding its fundamentals, technology, and market dynamics. Conduct thorough research and educate yourself before investing.

2. Investing More Than You Can Afford to Lose: Avoid investing more money than you can afford to lose. Bitcoin and cryptocurrencies are highly volatile assets, and prices can fluctuate dramatically. Only invest money that you're willing to risk.

3. Chasing Hype and FOMO (Fear of Missing Out): Avoid making investment decisions based on hype, media hype, or FOMO (fear of missing out). FOMO-driven investments often lead to buying at peak prices and panic selling during downturns.

4. Neglecting Risk Management: Neglecting risk management is a common mistake among investors. Always have a risk management strategy in place, including setting stop-loss orders, diversifying your portfolio, and avoiding excessive leverage.

5. Falling for Scams and Ponzi Schemes: Be wary of scams, Ponzi schemes, and fraudulent investment schemes in the cryptocurrency space. Exercise caution when approached with investment opportunities that promise guaranteed returns or seem too good to be true.

6. Ignoring Security Best Practices: Ignoring security best practices can result in loss of funds due to hacks, phishing attacks, or malware. Secure your Bitcoin holdings by using reputable wallets, enabling two-factor authentication (2FA), and keeping your private keys offline.

7. Emotional Investing: Emotional investing, driven by fear, greed, or panic, can lead to impulsive decisions and poor investment outcomes. Stay disciplined, stick to your investment plan, and avoid making decisions based on emotions.

8. Overtrading and Market Timing: Overtrading and attempting to time the market can lead to excessive trading fees, tax implications, and underperformance compared to a buy-and-hold strategy. Avoid frequent trading and focus on long-term investment goals.

9. Neglecting Tax Implications: Neglecting tax implications is a common mistake among investors. Be aware of tax obligations related to buying, selling, and holding Bitcoin, including capital gains taxes, income taxes, and reporting requirements.

10. Not Staying Informed: Not staying informed about news, trends, and developments in the cryptocurrency space can result in missed opportunities or uninformed investment decisions. Stay updated with market news, regulatory developments, and technological advancements.

Avoiding these common mistakes and practicing diligence, discipline, and sound investment principles, you can enhance your chances of success and navigate the challenges of investing in Bitcoin and cryptocurrencies effectively.

THE FUTURE OF BITCOIN AND CRYPTOCURRENCIES

The future of Bitcoin and cryptocurrencies is subject to various factors, including technological advancements, regulatory developments, market adoption, and macroeconomic trends. Here are some potential scenarios for the future of Bitcoin and cryptocurrencies:

1. Mainstream Adoption: Bitcoin and cryptocurrencies could achieve mainstream adoption as more individuals, institutions, and businesses recognize their potential as a store of value, medium of exchange, and investment asset. Increased adoption could lead to broader acceptance, integration into traditional financial systems, and greater use in everyday transactions.

2. Technological Innovation: Technological advancements, such as scalability improvements, privacy enhancements, and interoperability solutions, could address current limitations and make cryptocurrencies more efficient, user-friendly, and accessible. Innovations like the Lightning Network, second-layer protocols, and smart contract platforms could unlock new use cases and applications for cryptocurrencies beyond simple value transfer.

3. Regulatory Clarity: Clear and favorable regulatory frameworks could provide certainty and confidence to investors, businesses, and consumers, driving greater adoption and investment in cryptocurrencies. Regulatory clarity could also mitigate risks, address security concerns, and promote responsible innovation in the cryptocurrency ecosystem.

4. Financialization and Institutional Adoption: Increased financialization and institutional adoption of Bitcoin and cryptocurrencies could lead to the development of regulated investment products, such as exchange-traded funds (ETFs), futures contracts, and cryptocurrency custody services. Institutional involvement could bring liquidity, stability, and legitimacy to the cryptocurrency market, attracting a broader range of investors and capital.

5. Global Economic Uncertainty: Heightened geopolitical tensions, economic instability, and currency devaluation concerns could drive demand for non-inflationary assets like Bitcoin as a hedge against systemic risks and fiat currency depreciation. Bitcoin's finite supply, censorship resistance, and decentralized nature could appeal to individuals and investors seeking alternative stores of value and wealth preservation.

6. Interoperability and Integration: Increased interoperability and integration between different blockchain networks and cryptocurrencies could facilitate seamless asset transfers, cross-border payments, and decentralized finance (DeFi) applications. Interoperability protocols, cross-chain bridges, and atomic swaps could enable greater liquidity, efficiency, and accessibility in the cryptocurrency ecosystem.

7. Environmental Concerns and Sustainability: Environmental concerns related to Bitcoin's energy consumption and carbon footprint could prompt the development of more sustainable mining practices, energy-efficient consensus mechanisms, and renewable energy solutions. Efforts to address environmental impact could enhance Bitcoin's sustainability and long-term viability as a digital asset.

8. Social and Cultural Acceptance: Social and cultural acceptance of Bitcoin and cryptocurrencies could continue to grow as younger generations embrace digital assets, decentralized technologies, and financial sovereignty. Increased awareness, education, and advocacy could foster broader adoption and understanding of cryptocurrencies as tools for empowerment, inclusion, and economic freedom.

The future of Bitcoin and cryptocurrencies is dynamic and multifaceted, influenced by a wide range of technological, economic, regulatory, and social factors. While there are challenges and uncertainties ahead, the potential for innovation, disruption, and positive impact remains significant in shaping the future of finance and digital assets.

PREPARING FOR THE LONG HAUL

Preparing for the long haul when investing in Bitcoin and cryptocurrencies requires a combination of strategic planning, risk management, and patience. Here's how you can prepare for the long term:

1. Understand the Technology: Educate yourself about the underlying technology behind Bitcoin and cryptocurrencies, including blockchain technology, consensus mechanisms, and cryptographic principles. Understanding the technology can help you appreciate its long-term potential and value proposition.

2. Set Clear Goals: Define your investment goals and objectives for the long term. Determine your investment horizon, risk tolerance, and desired outcomes. Whether you're investing for retirement, wealth preservation, or financial independence, having clear goals can guide your investment strategy and decision-making process.

3. Diversify Your Portfolio: Diversify your investment portfolio across different asset classes, sectors, and geographic regions to spread risk and minimize exposure to any single investment. Consider allocating a portion of your portfolio to Bitcoin and cryptocurrencies as part of a diversified investment strategy.

4. Invest for the Long Term: Take a long-term perspective when investing in Bitcoin and cryptocurrencies. Avoid succumbing to short-term market volatility or price fluctuations and focus on the fundamentals and long-term potential of the assets you're investing in.

5. Practice Dollar-Cost Averaging (DCA): Implement a dollar-cost averaging strategy by investing a fixed amount of money into Bitcoin or cryptocurrencies at regular intervals (e.g., weekly, monthly). DCA can help smooth out market volatility and reduce the risk of mistiming the market.

6. Stay Informed and Educated: Stay informed about news, trends, and developments in the cryptocurrency space. Keep track of technological advancements, regulatory developments, and market trends that may impact the long-term prospects of Bitcoin and cryptocurrencies.

7. Practice Patience and Discipline: Practice patience and discipline when investing for the long term. Avoid making impulsive decisions based on short-term market movements or emotional reactions. Stick to your investment plan and remain committed to your long-term goals.

8. Rebalance Your Portfolio Periodically: Periodically review and rebalance your investment portfolio to ensure it remains aligned with your long-term goals and risk tolerance. Rebalancing involves selling assets that have appreciated in value and reallocating funds to assets that may be undervalued or underrepresented in your portfolio.

9. Consider Tax Implications: Consider the tax implications of your investment decisions, including capital gains taxes, income taxes, and reporting requirements related to buying, selling, and holding Bitcoin and cryptocurrencies. Consult with a tax advisor or accountant to optimize your tax strategy and minimize tax liabilities.

10. Secure Your Investments: Secure your Bitcoin and cryptocurrency investments by using reputable wallets, implementing best security practices, and safeguarding your private keys. Protecting your investments from theft, hacking, or loss is essential for long-term wealth preservation.

Following these steps and adopting a disciplined, long-term investment approach, you can better position yourself to navigate the ups and downs of the cryptocurrency market and achieve your financial goals over time.

CONCLUSION

Investing in Bitcoin and cryptocurrencies can be both exciting and rewarding, but it also comes with risks and uncertainties. As we've explored, Bitcoin has the potential to revolutionize finance, reshape industries, and empower individuals with financial sovereignty. However, success in the cryptocurrency market requires careful planning, strategic thinking, and disciplined execution.

Throughout this journey, we've discussed the fundamentals of Bitcoin, explored investment strategies, and highlighted the importance of risk management and staying informed. Whether you're a beginner or an experienced investor, the key to long-term success lies in understanding the technology, setting clear goals, and being patient and disciplined in your approach.

As you prepare for the long haul, remember to diversify your portfolio, invest for the long term, and stay informed about market trends and developments. Be mindful of common mistakes to avoid, such as investing more than you can afford to lose, chasing hype, and neglecting security best practices.

In the dynamic and ever-evolving world of Bitcoin and cryptocurrencies, adaptability, resilience, and continuous learning are essential. Embrace the opportunities, but also remain vigilant and cautious. By taking a thoughtful and measured approach to investing, you can navigate the challenges and uncertainties of the cryptocurrency market and position yourself for long-term success.

Ultimately, the future of Bitcoin and cryptocurrencies holds immense potential, but it's up to each of us to seize the opportunities and navigate the complexities of this emerging asset class. As you embark on your investment journey, may you find success, fulfillment, and prosperity in the world of digital assets.

www.ingramcontent.com/pod-product-compliance
Lightning Source LLC
Chambersburg PA
CBHW070113230526
45472CB00004B/1235